CRUISIN'

Dragsters

By Maureen Connolly

111069

PUBLISHED BY
Capstone Press
Mankato, Minnesota USA

CIP
LIBRARY OF CONGRESS CATALOGING IN PUBLICATION DATA

Connolly, Maureen A.
  Dragsters / Maureen A. Connolly.
      p. cm. — (Cruisin')
  Summary: Describes the history of drag racing, the characteristics of different kinds of dragsters, racing rules, and drag racing events.

  ISBN 1-56065-074-5:
  1. Automobiles. Racing—Juvenile literature. 2. Drag racing—Juvenile literature. [1. Automobiles, Racing. 2. Drag racing.]
  I. Title. II. Series.
  TL236.C593   1990
  796.7—dc20   89-39674
                                            CIP
                                            AC

Photo Credits:
John Asher

Capstone Press
P.O. Box 669, Mankato, MN, U.S.A. 56002-0669

Jim Murphy's Dodge with the body down and latched, ready to race

A full roll cage with driver ready. Shows full-face helmet, eye-hole balaclava (fire protection beneath helmet), and the neck collar beneath the helmet to avoid neck injuries.

CONTENTS

Two stock eliminator cars do their burnouts side by side before racing.

THE RACE IS ON!

Some of the fastest and most powerful cars today are dragsters. There are many types of dragsters. Some look like regular cars. Some are far-out vehicles that you will never see on the street. Dragsters can travel nearly 300 miles an hour on special tracks called **drag strips**.

Drag racing is one of the most thrilling kinds of automobile racing. It's a sport with lots of color, noise, and excitement. In a drag race only two dragsters race against each other. The first dragster to cross the finish line wins. The winner is the **eliminator**. Sometimes the winner crosses the finish line one-tenth of a second before the loser. That is just about the blink of an eye.

Get ready. Get set. The drag race is on!

THE HISTORY OF DRAGSTERS

The first dragsters were raced by teenagers on the streets of Southern California more than 50 years ago. Teenagers took regular cars and made them faster and more powerful. The teenagers called their cars hot rods. Two hot rods pulled up beside each other, one driver signaled, both cars raced off in a cloud of smoke. Racing hot rods in the street was dangerous and illegal.

Many teenagers took their hot rods to dry lake beds, deserts, and old airports. Eventually drag strips were built just for racing.

In 1951, racers formed the National Hot Rod Association to set the rules for drag racing. Soon drag racing became popular, and hot rods became known as dragsters.

Norm Wizner's "Jukebox Ford" is a 1956 Crown Victoria model with a fiberglass body covering a very sophisticated chassis and a 700-cubic-inch engine. This car runs over 200 miles per hour.

Top Fuel driver Maurice Dupont

Fuel-injected small-block Chevrolet using gasoline

INSIDE DRAGSTERS

A dragster needs special equipment to do its job. Some dragsters are built just for racing. Others are regular cars that have been changed for drag racing. These changes improve the performance of the vehicle. A dragster can be called **modified** or **altered**. An altered dragster has been changed more than a modified dragster.

Dragsters travel so fast they need help stopping. Many dragsters use parachutes to slow down. The parachute is made of strong nylon and is folded up in a package that looks like a backpack. It is located behind the driver's head. The driver pulls a cable to release the parachute. In drag racing, opening the parachute is called **popping the chute**. It's also known as **hanging out the laundry**. After the dragster slows down, the driver hits the brakes to stop.

Engines

A dragster needs a hefty engine to accelerate fast. The engine's power is measured in **horsepower**. Dragster engines can have 4,000 horsepower. Regular cars have about 150 horsepower.

A dragster has an **internal combustion engine**. An internal combustion engine has **cylinders**. Fuel burns in the cylinders, and the engine gets its power from burning the fuel. Most dragsters have cylinders that are pipe-shaped with flat tops. Some dragsters have a type of cylinder called a **hemi**. A hemi has a round top and can burn more fuel to give the engine more power. Many dragsters have extra cylinders for extra energy.

When the driver steps on a pedal, called the **throttle**, fuel goes to the engine. A dragster moving at top power and top speed is going full throttle.

A dragster can have special equipment to boost the power of the engine. A **fuel injection system** forces fuel into each cylinder and gives the dragster steady power.

A dragster can be supercharged to accelerate quickly and reach very high speeds in a few seconds. A **blower** is a supercharger that gives the engine extra power by forcing air into the cylinders.

A dragster engine produces **exhaust** when it burns fuel. The exhaust system, or **headers**, takes the gases from combustion out of the dragster. Some dragsters use their exhaust to run a **turbocharger**. A turbocharger is another kind of blower. A turbocharger also forces air into the cylinders to make the engine more efficient.

The **transmission** sends power from the dragster engine through **gears** to the wheels. A dragster can have a standard transmission or an automatic transmission. A standard transmission has a **clutch** and a **shifter**, also called the stick. The driver operates the clutch and shifter together to increase or decrease power and to move the dragster forward or backward. A dragster with an automatic transmission has only a shifter.

Fuel-injected big-block Chevrolet using gasoline fuel

Wheels

Dragsters need good **traction** to accelerate rapidly. Unusual tires called **slicks** are put on their rear wheels. Slicks are made from soft, sticky rubber and have a flat surface and no treads. Slicks are about three feet high and a foot and a half wide. Some dragsters use motorcycle tires on the front wheels. Other dragsters use regular car tires on the front.

Many dragsters have **wheelie bars**. They are small wheels behind the slicks to prevent the dragster from tipping backward at high speed.

Wheelie bars are mounted to the rear end of the race car.

Chassis and Bodies

The **chassis** is the frame of the dragster. The engine, wheels, brakes, and other parts are added to the chassis. A dragster can have a **reinforced** chassis.

The **body** covers the chassis and is made of metal, fiberglass or plastic. The dragster's body is usually painted with bright colors and may be decorated with decals and bumper stickers. Drivers usually paint their own names on the doors or hood of their dragsters. Drag racers also give their dragsters special names like *Red Devil, Big Trouble,* or *Hot Shot.*

Driver's name appears on side of car

TOP FUEL DRAGSTERS

Top Fuel Dragsters are also called Top Fuel Eliminators. Their nicknames are **rails**, **diggers**, and **slingshots**. They burn nitro. They are the superstars of drag racing.

Top Fuelers are the only dragsters that don't look like regular cars. They are built just for drag racing. They are only good at going a short distance in a straight line at high speed. A Top Fueler can run the quarter mile in 4.9 seconds at 294 miles per hour.

A Top Fueler is long and skinny. It is nearly 25 feet long, or about twice as long as a regular car. It is three feet wide and only three feet high. The front is narrower than the rear. It weighs about 2000 pounds.

A Top Fueler has a chassis made of strong steel. The body is made of fiberglass or plastic, and it has no fenders or bumpers. It does have a metal **push bar** in the back because the big engine cannot start by itself. It must be pushed to the starting line by a car or a truck and has to be towed off the drag strip after a race.

Usually an **airfoil** is on the rear of a Top Fueler, and some have a **spoiler** on the front. Airfoils and spoilers resemble airplane wings and keep the Top Fueler down on the track.

Top Fuel driver Kenny Bernstein climbs into the seat as the engine is warmed up in the pits after being worked on between rounds of racing.

A Top Fueler engine can be over 4,000 horsepower. The engine is made of aluminum and is specially built for racing. It is fuel injected and supercharged. Most transmissions have one forward gear and one reverse gear. The engine is in the back between the rear wheels. Top Fuelers have huge rear slicks. The front wheels are smaller. They are about 13 inches high, with spokes like motorcycle wheels.

A Top Fueler has brakes on the back wheels, but not on the front wheels. Stopping is difficult and a chute is necessary to slow down. Some Top Fuelers have two chutes.

The driver sits in the **cockpit**, just in front of the engine. The controls are in the cockpit with a steering wheel shaped like a butterfly. The cockpit is small and narrow. The driver is only a few inches off the ground, practically lying down. A **roll bar** is over the driver's head. A cushion about four inches behind the driver's head gives extra protection.

Top Fuelers are some of the world's most expensive vehicles. A Top Fueler can cost more than $100,000.

Ed "The Ace" McCulloch was one of the winningest Funny Car drivers in the world, but is shown here racing in a Top Fueler.

The engine is being started.

The starter motor has been removed and the body pole taken away so the body is lowered and latched closed.

FUNNY CARS

Funny Cars are serious dragsters. Drag racing fans are crazy about them. On the outside, a Funny Car looks like an ordinary car. On the inside, a Funny Car is really a Top Fueler. It never goes in the street and is legal only on the drag strip.

The body of a Funny Car is made of fiberglass or plastic. The doors, windows, hood, and trunk do not open. They are all fake. Even the headlights are fake. A Funny Car usually has holes in the hood for a supercharger.

The Funny Car body opens like a giant clam. It is a flip-top car. Inside is a frame that is a little smaller than a Top Fueler frame. The engine is also like a Top Fueler engine. It can burn nitro, alcohol, or gas and is in the front of the Funny Car. The driver sits in a bucket seat where the back seat is supposed to be and uses a small steering wheel. A roll bar protects the driver from injuries.

The driver is not able to jump in or out of the Funny Car. The whole top must be lifted off. It does have an escape hatch in the roof for the driver to use in an emergency.

The front tires are usually smaller than the rear slicks and are about the size of regular car tires. Just like Top Fuelers, Funny Cars have wheelie bars on the back.

It has front and rear brakes and it needs at least one chute to come to a stop.

The front end points down, and the body is about two inches shorter than a regular car body. A Funny Car is **raked** and **chopped** to move faster. It shakes a lot and is difficult to handle. The front also lifts at high speeds. Some Funny Cars travel faster than Top Fuelers, but most are slower. A Funny Car is less than a second behind a Top Fueler and can travel more than 290 miles per hour. The engine has more than 3,000 horsepower. A Funny Car can cost nearly as much as a Top Fueler.

The car moves forward toward the start.

Dennis Taylor blasts off the starting line carrying the front end in the air.

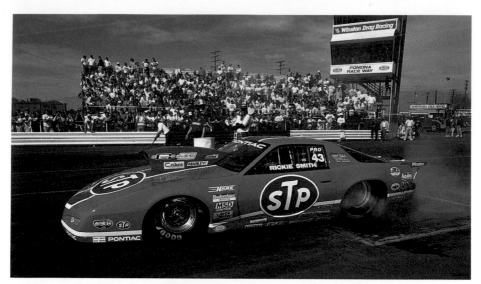

Rickie Smith of King, North Carolina, drives the "STP Pontiac" and has won five World Championships in International Hot Rod Association (IHRA) Competition.

Jerry Eckman and car owner Bill Orndoff will be hard to beat on the track.

PRO STOCKS

Pro Stock cars are more like regular cars than Top Fuelers or Funny Cars. Pro Stockers look like regular cars but are rebuilt to make them more powerful. Sometimes they are called **Muscle Cars**. A Pro Stock car can go more than 193 miles per hour. It runs the drag strip in about 7 seconds.

The body of the Pro Stock car is steel. Sometimes the body is dipped in acid to make it smoother. The front fenders, hood, and trunk are plastic. Inside, most of the instruments on the dashboard are just painted on. All of these changes make the Pro Stock car lighter so that it can travel faster, but also make Pro Stockers very expensive.

The driver of the Pro Stock car sits in the usual driver's seat. The car has many safety features to protect the driver. It has a **roll cage** and a roll bar. The driver wears a safety harness. A Pro Stock car has a windshield and windows. The glass is safety glass and will not injure the driver if it breaks in an accident. A Pro Stock car burns alcohol or gasoline.

Just as there are many different car models on the street, there are many models of Pro Stock cars. They are put in groups according to their make, weight, horsepower, and transmission. A Pro Stock car must be a car built recently in North America. It can have more than one engine, but the engines must be made in North America. Similar cars race against each other.

Pro Stock cars look like cars of the future. Pro Stockers are the cars many fans dream about.

Jim Yates was the runner-up at the 1992 NHRA Winter-nationals with his Dynomax Pontiac.

DRAG STRIP RACING

Drag racing is safer than many kinds of automobile racing. Yet it has many dangers. The big engines of dragsters are pushed to their limits on the drag strip. They can explode or catch fire. A **blow-up** is when an engine explodes. In a blow-up, parts of the dragster engine or body can scatter over the drag strip. Many dragsters have a thick metal shield to separate the driver from the engine. In a blow-up, the shield prevents parts from hitting the driver.

Fire is always a hazard on the drag strip. Engines can burst into flames. Some dragsters have fire walls to keep flames away from the driver. Dragsters have built-in fire extinguishers that go off automatically. The driver can also start the extinguishers by pulling a cable. The extinguishers spray the engine and the driver with Halon to stop the flames.

Dragsters can roll over or crash. A roll cage made of steel and welded onto the chassis protects the driver in case of an accident. The driver sits inside the roll cage. Many dragsters have a heavy metal pipe called a roll bar that curves over the driver's head. The inside of the dragster can have soft padding to protect the driver.

Fairplex Park, Pomona, California, home of the Winter-nationals and Winston Finals.

Every drag racer knows the importance of safety. Drivers always wear helmets and use seat belts or safety harnesses. Drivers wear goggles for extra protection and gas masks to filter out harmful fumes. Many drivers wear fire-proof jumpsuits that resemble astronaut clothing. For extra protection, they wear heavy boots, gloves, and long underwear that are fire-proof. Some drivers wear a fire-proof face mask with a slit for the eyes.

A drag strip is the only place to see dragsters at work. Most drag strips are a quarter of a mile long. A quarter of a mile is a good distance for a drag race because the dragster has room to go full throttle. It is also a distance that doesn't strain the engine.

All drag strips are straight and paved like a highway with at least two lanes for racing. The track must be kept clean. Fuel, oil, auto parts, and dirt on the drag strip can endanger the dragsters.

The lanes are marked by painted lines or separated by a fence or guard rail. Each lane has a starting line and a finish line. The drag strip has a third lane that the dragsters use to get back to the starting line after a race. The **shutdown strip**, or the **overrun**, is at the end of the drag strip. Dragsters use the shutdown strip to come to a stop after the race.

The **pits** are where the dragsters park between races. The pits are filled with dragsters, drivers, mechanics, engine parts, tools, and tow trucks. The pits have sections for each kind of dragster.

The **staging area** is where the dragsters **rev** up their engines and get ready to move to the starting line. The staging area has a **burn-out pit**, a small section of pavement with a puddle of water. This area is also called the **bleach box** because dragsters once used a puddle of laundry bleach. Dragsters spin their wheels in the puddle to clean and heat up the rubber, giving the slicks better traction.

Drag racing uses electronic equipment to start and to end each race. The **Christmas Tree** is a pole of colored lights about 20 feet from the starting line. The tree stands between the two lanes, and each dragster has its own row of lights.

The top light of the tree, the **pre-staging light**, is small and amber. When it goes off, the dragster moves toward the starting line. The second light, also small and amber, is the **staging light**. It goes off when the dragster is on the starting line. The next three lights are also amber, but are larger. They are the **starting lights,** or the countdown lights, that blink every half second to tell the driver to get ready. The next light is green and tells the driver to go. The bottom light is red and is the foul light. It flashes if the driver starts too soon.

The tree also has a large blue light near the top. It is a warning light that tells the driver the car has rolled over the starting line before the race begins.

Drivers and fans need to know which dragster won the race and how fast each dragster traveled. The drag strip uses a photoelectric beam to determine the winner of the race and the speeds of both dragsters. The green light on the tree starts a clock for the race. The first dragster to drive across the photoelectric beam at the finish line stops the clock.

The drag strip also has a **speed trap** with two photoelectric beams to measure speed. One beam is 66 feet after the starting line. The other is 66 feet before the finish line. When a dragster goes through the beams, an instrument measures its speed.

A front view of the Christmas Tree

HOW DRAG RACES ARE RUN

A day of drag races is called a **drag meet**. Each race is called an **elimination** or a **heat**. The winner of each heat goes on to face another dragster. At the end of the day, each class of dragsters has one eliminator.

At the start of the drag meet, race officials carefully inspect the dragsters. They weigh each dragster and check to be sure that it is safe. The race officials also make sure that each driver knows the rules of drag racing.

Every dragster gets two numbers. One number identifies the class the dragster races in so that only similar dragsters race against each other. The second number identifies the driver. Drivers paint the numbers on the windows of the dragsters in washable paint or use decals.

At race time, the dragsters move from the pits to the staging area. The announcer calls two dragsters to the starting line. The dragsters stop at the burn-out pit and gun their engines. The tires spin. They make a cloud of hot, smelly rubber. Then the dragsters inch toward the starting line.

Tony Foti is part of a Los Angeles Police Department program to help keep kids off drugs and in school. His supercharged Chevrolet generally makes exhibition runs, but could compete in the Super comp class, where it can run no quicker than 8.90 seconds.

Don Keen's Mustang does a burnout prior to racing in Stock Eliminator. Don won the Division 7 title in 1991 and finished number 3 in the world rankings.

*Buddy Nickens won Super Stock at the Arizona Nationals.
Buddy has learned to expect the green!*

The start must be carefully controlled. Professional dragsters have a **heads-up start**. They start at the same time. Amateur drivers have a **handicap start**. One dragster gets to start a split second before the other.

A race official called a **starter** stands between the two dragsters and pushes a button to start the Christmas Tree. Drag races are won or lost at the starting line. The drivers know they have to start the instant the green light flashes. Winning drivers have learned to expect the green.

A dragster leaves the starting line in a smoke-filled roar known as the launch. A dragster that races down the strip with the engine at peak performance makes a **perfect run**.

Drag races are measured in **elapsed time**, or **E.T.**, for short. Elapsed time is how long it takes a car to go from the starting line to the finish line. After every race, officials give each driver a piece of paper with the elapsed time for the race. Drivers are also told their speed.

Speed is not always important. All that matters is getting to the finish line first. Drag racers say that the fastest dragster may not be the quickest dragster. A dragster that gets a late start cannot win no matter how fast it goes.

DRAGSTER DRIVERS

Drivers have to know every inch of their dragsters. They have to think and act fast and cannot make a mistake on the drag strip. Most drivers are amateurs. Only a few are professionals. Drivers are called **drag racers**, **rodders**, **hands**, or **shoes**. The best drivers are called **hot shoes**.

A driver needs training, a regular driver's license, and a competition license. That license shows that the driver knows the rules of drag racing and has learned to drive safely. Top Fueler and Funny Car drivers may need to pass a difficult test to qualify for the fastest races. Those drivers have to show they can find the controls in their dragsters even when wearing blindfolds.

A racing team in action. Four-time Winston World Champion Joe Amato has already completed his burnout in his Valvoline Special, and as the car approaches the starting line, each member of the unit is assigned a specific task. The man reaching beneath the front of the car is turning on the computer that will record the car's every action during the run.

WRENCHES AND RACING TEAMS

Drivers get most of the attention at the drag strip. But drivers are only part of the team needed to run a winning dragster. A racing team keeps the dragster in top condition.

In drag racing, mechanics are called **wrenches**. The top mechanic is the **chief wrench**. A wrench keeps the dragster in good working condition and makes sure the dragster is safe.

Wrenches work in the pits and can rebuild an engine in only minutes. Wrenches tune the engine, put in fuel, repair and replace broken parts. They also change the tires and keep the dragster clean and polished.

Most amateur drivers work on their own dragsters, while professional drivers have many wrenches to maintain their dragsters. Drag racers depend on their wrenches and sometimes even paint the name of the chief wrench on the side of the dragster. Wrenches from different teams often help out each other when problems occur. Some dragsters have on-board computers to show the driver how the engine is running. Teams also use computers before or after a race to check for mechanical problems.

LEARN MORE ABOUT DRAGSTERS

You can find out more about dragsters and drag racing at your library or book store. Some of the magazines about drag racing are *National Dragster, Hot Rod,* and *Hot Rodding.* You can also see drag racing on television, but the best place to learn about drag racing is at a drag strip. There are hundreds of drag strips in the United States and Canada. At the drag strip, you can see different kinds of dragsters, visit the pits, talk to drivers and wrenches, and experience the thrill and excitement of drag racing.

A happy moment for a racer and his team. Mark Pawuk's group earned a $3000 bonus for being the Number 1 qualifiers in Pro Stock at the Winternationals.

Dragster drivers must have arm restraint straps to help keep their arms and hands within the confines of the roll cage if the car turns over.

GLOSSARY

Airfoil: a flat or curved piece on the rear of the car that air moves through to help control the dragster.

Altered: changed or modified to make different.

Bleach box: old name for the burn-out pit, where dragsters spin their tires before the race.

Blow-up: when an engine explodes.

Blower: a supercharger that gives the engine more power.

Body: the covering that goes over the chassis.

Burn-out pit: a small section of pavement in the staging area with a puddle of water where dragsters spin their tires.

Chassis: the frame of the dragster.

Chief wrench: the head mechanic on a racing team.

Chopped: cut shorter.

Christmas Tree: a pole with the colored lights used for the drag races.

Clutch: the part of the standard transmission that the driver operates to increase or decrease the power of the dragster.

Cockpit: where the driver sits.

Cylinders: the pipe-shaped chambers that burn the fuel and give the engine power.

Diggers: nickname for a Top Fuel dragster.

Drag meet: a day of racing.

Drag racers: the drivers.

Drag strips: the tracks used for dragsters.

Elapsed time or **E.T.**: the time it takes a dragster to go from the starting line to the finish line.

Elimination: each drag race or heat.

Eliminator: the winner of a drag race.

Exhaust: the fumes from the burning of the fuel.

Fuel injection system: forces fuel into the cylinders to make the dragster more powerful.

Gears: devices that move power from the engine to the wheels.

Handicap start: used when amateur drivers are racing. One driver starts a split second before the other.

Hands: another nickname for the drivers.

Hanging out the laundry: the opening of the parachute to slow down a dragster.

Headers: the pipe or tube that allows the exhaust to flow out of the dragster.

Heads-up start: when the drivers start the race at the same time. Used in professional races.

Heat: each race during a drag meet.

Hemi: a cylinder with a round top that burns more fuel and gives the engine more power.

Horsepower: the unit of measure used to measure the power of engines or motors.

Hot shoes: a nickname for the best drivers.

Internal combustion engine: an engine in which the power is created by the explosion of a mixture of the fuel and air in the cylinders.

Modified: altered or changed.

Muscle Cars: Pro Stock dragsters.

Overrun: the strip at the end of a dragstrip.

Perfect run: when a dragster makes it down the drag strip with the engine at peak performance.

Pits: where dragsters park between races.

Popping the chute: when the parachute opens to slow down the dragster.

Pre-staging light: the small, amber light at the top of the Christmas Tree. Tells the drivers to move toward the starting line.

Push bar: a metal bar on the back of the dragster used to push the dragster to the starting line or remove it from the track.

Rails: Top Fuel dragsters.

Raked: designed so that the front of the dragster points down to the track instead of in the wind.

Reinforced: strengthened.

Rev: to accelerate.

Rodders: nickname for drivers of dragsters.

Roll bar: a heavy metal pipe that curves over the driver's head.

Roll cage: a cage made out of steel to protect the driver in case of an accident.

Shifter: the stick used to change the speed or direction of the dragster.

Shoes: drivers of dragsters.

Shutdown strip: the strip at the end of the drag strip.

Slicks: the rear tires on dragsters.

Slingshots: Top Fuel dragsters.

Speed trap: used to measure the speed of the dragsters in a race.

Spoiler: resembles an airplane wing on the front of the dragster to help control the dragster.

Staging area: where dragsters rev up their engines before moving to the starting line.

Staging light: the second light on the Christmas Tree. It is small and amber and goes off when the dragster is on the starting line.

Starter: a race official.

Starting lights: three large amber lights on the Christmas Tree that blink every half second to tell the driver to get ready.

Throttle: the valve that regulates the amount of fuel going into the cylinders.

Traction: adhesive friction.

Transmission: sends power from the engine through the gears.

Turbocharger: a blower that forces air into the cylinders to make the engine more efficient.

Wheelie bars: the small wheels behind the rear slicks that prevent the dragster from tipping backward at high speed.

Wrenches: mechanics that work on the dragsters.

INDEX